BREAKING
THROUGH
in prayer

freshwind
publishing

ASH KOTECHA

Contents

Dedication

I would like to dedicate this booklet to my life
partner Sharon, who first helped in my journey
of prayer, and my incredible daughter Esther
who has put all of this together.

1

How I learnt to Pray Through

1985 was the year I started my new job working alongside my Pastor. He gave me my first project which was to organise the transport of our visitors from America. We had a team of twenty young people coming to Gatwick Airport and my responsibility was to send the minibus to Gatwick to collect them. On the same day but on a different flight, the American Pastor and his wife were coming to Heathrow Airport and I was to send a car to pick them up.

It was a very simple task and the secretary in America had sent the flight details, i.e. the time of arrival of each flight to Gatwick and Heathrow, and yet I was worried sick! I was newly married and my wife Sharon noticed how worried I was. I still had two weeks before the visitors arrived and every day I worried because this was my very first assignment and obviously I didn't want to mess up my new job, though it was hard to see how I could possibly get things wrong.

Sharon suggested I should pray it all through. Pray? I had never realised that these things could be covered in prayer, and anyhow to cut a long story short I started to pray in tongues almost all the time I thought about worrying! After a few days of panic-praying in tongues I noticed the wonderful sense of being in a bubble, and I knew everything would be alright. Deep down inside me I felt God's peace settling in. Finally the day arrived to send the two vehicles out to the two airports. I made quite sure the evening before that I had given the driver of the minibus all the flight details to go to Gatwick, and the other driver with the BMW was given instructions to go to Heathrow.

Several times I told them all the details and made sure they had understood it all. They had to get up quite early to ensure they avoided the rush hour traffic and be there for our visitors on time - what could possibly go wrong? But I was in for a surprise! Early next morning the phone rang and it was one of the drivers calling from the airport. He had the minibus and was supposed to go to Gatwick airport but for some unknown reason he'd gone to Heathrow and the driver of the BMW who was supposed to pick up the pastor and his wife from Heathrow ended up going to Gatwick. What a mess!

I was panicking! How could they possibly make such a mistake? Again, to cut a long story short, it turned out that the secretary in America had got things the wrong way round, which meant I had the right vehicle in place at the right airport! I simply could not believe that the mistake the drivers had made was necessary in order to be at the right place at the right time! Only God knew that the secretary would get things the wrong way round, and only God caused both drivers to go to the airport where they would be needed. I never revealed to anyone the mess which turned out to be my message on prayer. Since that day over thirty years ago, I started to pray daily, and if there was a project or issue or situation, my wife and I would pray it through!

We learnt to pray through in tongues for all our difficulties, challenges and obstacles in our lives and the lives of others and saw God answer our prayer, known as the prayer of intercession, and we did not stop until we had broken through to that place of peace or knew deep down that all was well, even though in the natural realm it seemed nothing had changed. I learnt to win the battle in the spirit realm first to see the outcome manifest in the natural realm. We prayed through times of sickness, financial hardship and received direction from the Lord. My journey into intercessory prayer had begun, and still to this day I pray daily with my wife at least an hour a day in tongues (Matthew 26:40).

2

Jackie Pullinger

As a young Christian I loved reading Christian testimonies, and one of them is the famous story of Jackie Pullinger called *Chasing the Dragon*. She became a missionary to the Walled City in Hong Kong where gangsters and drug-addicts thrived. She came to a point in her ministry to the drug addicts that no-one was listening to her, and her ministry was pretty ineffectual.

Eventually she got baptised in the Holy Spirit and started speaking in tongues. As she started praying in the Spirit she noticed a remarkable change in her ministry. The drug addicts started getting saved and baptised in the Holy Spirit, so she prayed all day long in tongues from then on. Her ministry blossomed and she learnt the secret to transforming lives. Also she observed that the drug addicts were able to come off drugs by praying in tongues, and they did not suffer the terrible withdrawal symptoms which would otherwise accompany this process. If praying in tongues could deliver and set free even drug addicts, I was convinced that I must also continue in this vein. Her testimony inspired me to continue praying in tongues.

The second book that helped me was a book by Dr. Paul Yonggi Cho from South Korea called *Prayer, the Key to Revival.* He talked about 'praying through' and building up your prayer account. People always asked Dr. Cho about his phenomenal success in ministry, building a church of nearly a million people which he attributes to the power of praying in the Holy Spirit!

One of the stories he told really inspired me. In the 1970's when he was involved in a building project, the oil prices had gone up, people started losing their jobs, and the income of the church fell dramatically. He needed five million dollars to finish the new church building. It was a lot of money to find and he was in a terrible place financially, so all he could do is look to God and pray in tongues. He prayed like a mad man, often during the night, praying in tongues for five million dollars. It was a gigantic mountain to climb but he kept praying in the Spirit. He knew he needed to get his miracle in the Spirit first before it materialised in the natural realm. After several months of incessant prayer, one day getting out of bed, the 'heavens opened up' and he knew God had granted him the five million dollars.

Even though he had no money in the bank, he knew that he knew he would get the money somehow. The bank came through for him and lent him the money without collateral, and those were the days when no-one was lending money in South Korea. He was able to finish the building, the country's economy began to improve, people started getting jobs and he was able to pay back the loan.

King of The Universe

Dr. Cho I learnt is a great man of prayer, and though he has handed over the position of Senior Pastor of his church now, he continues to work for the Lord and no doubt continues to pray much. As head pastor he used to spend his first three hours at the office in prayer. He told his secretary that no-one was to disturb him during those first three hours of the day, no matter how urgent the situation. The secretary had strict orders that Dr. Cho would not talk to anyone until he had finished his morning prayer time. One day the President of South Korea who always admired Dr. Cho telephoned for some advice, but the secretary explained that Dr. Cho was in prayer and could not be disturbed. "This is the President of South Korea," he shouted, but the secretary would still not put his call through. Finally when Dr. Cho came out of his prayer time, he called the President to find out the problem. "Why couldn't your secretary put me through to your office?" the President complained, "doesn't she realise I am the President of South Korea?" Dr Cho replied calmly and said, "You may be the President of South Korea but I must follow full protocol - I was talking to the King of the Universe who has priority over my time!"

My faith began to grow in the area of prayer and intercession until I knew I had the answer in my spirit. I realised that when I broke through in prayer I would have a tremendous peace, sometimes a wonderful sense of joy and well-being, knowing within my heart that I had touched God in prayer and the answer was on its way. Such knowledge and understanding took time to develop, but soon I was learning to pray through situations, and time after time I saw God's answer to prayer.

It was not a case of hit or miss, but certain confidence deep within that all was well! God was calling me into the ministry but I was reluctant because I preferred earning a living and having a normal life, and so I became involved in a little business venture which failed. We were absolutely broke, so much so that we didn't even have money for food. My rent which was forty pounds per week was also due, and we were in a desperate situation. I didn't want to ask anyone for help so I started to pray in tongues. I had no other option but to pray. Sharon had a part-time job but her money was not due yet and we needed the money immediately.

While she was at work I prayed in tongues continuously for hours. After a few days of constant prayer there was a knock on my door and a wealthy woman (who used to come to our church) stood outside in her fur coat. She said, "Ash, please stop praying for I can hear you!" (How could she hear me praying? She lived five miles away!) She handed me an envelope which had three hundred pounds in it (that was a lot of money for us in those days). With that I was able to pay the rent, buy some groceries and I banked the rest of the money. I had prayed through in tongues and God supplied my need through this wealthy woman. She lived five miles away but God caused her to hear my prayer for finances! Amazing!

It was soon after, I realised I needed to obey God and join the church's ministry staff, where I soon was leading the Tuesday night prayer meeting and hundreds came to pray in those days.

Miracle Pregnancy

I have many such testimonies of answered prayer, but I will relate this next story which I feel will encourage you to also become a person of prayer. When Sharon was expecting our one and only child she started to bleed (at 14 weeks), and we rushed to the hospital as the situation looked critical for the baby. Sharon was hooked up to some tubes and I left her around 6pm to come home to rest. I couldn't rest or eat as I was so on edge. This was a miracle pregnancy as we had waited over five years for Sharon to conceive and we didn't want to lose this baby - all I could do is pray in tongues! Needless to say I was panic-praying, and I prayed and prayed in tongues because I didn't know what else to do. I remembered having interceded for a few hours and suddenly around 11pm I broke through!

I knew without a shadow of a doubt that everything was going to be alright, and as my head hit the pillow I fell sound asleep. The next morning I rushed over to the hospital to find Sharon looking very normal and she told me the tubes had fallen out in the middle of the night. I knew God had taken care of everything so I told her we were going home.

The nurse said we should not go, but I told her that Sharon was fine (and she was fine) and we went home. We continued praying in tongues everyday for a safe delivery for the baby, and the day finally arrived for her to give birth. I knew the baby was coming at the start of Sharon's labour pains but the nurse said no, she's still too early yet so please go home. I stood my ground until the junior doctor arrived.

He said the same thing, go home, it's not time for the baby to come, but I had been in prayer for many weeks and I knew the baby was due this day. Finally the consultant was called in and he examined Sharon and said to the nurse - what are you waiting for, this baby is coming now! Four and a half hours later, our daughter Esther was born. At the time of writing this she is now 21 years old but this testimony still stays with me!

3

Angels on assignment

In Acts 12:5 we read how Herod the King killed James, the brother of John and then took Peter prisoner as well. The Church lost James but they did not want to lose Peter as well, and so the whole Church started to pray.

Peter was therefore kept in prison, but constant prayer was offered to God for him by the church.

Here it says that the Church prayed constantly and they prayed through until God sent His angel who brought about his escape from prison — quite an amazing story and it's one of my favourites. James lost his life, but Peter was delivered because the church prayed relentlessly. Although it does not tell us how they prayed, I am sure they included praying in tongues because if you are praying in your own language you soon run out of things to say!

Another example of angelic intervention was when the Apostle Paul was in a ship on his way to Rome to appear before Caesar. In Acts 27:21-24 it describes how the prisoners and crew had been caught in a storm and would have perished but for Paul's prayers.

Even though God had told Paul that he must go to Rome, he would not have made it without divine intervention because the captain of the ship did not listen to Paul's warning. God revealed to him in advance that the ship would be in danger, and so for many days Paul fasted and prayed, and an angel was sent by God to save the ship and all on board, and so even though shipwrecked they landed on the island of Malta. We know how the gospel came to Malta — it was through the Apostle Paul.

The war in the heavenlies

In the Old Testament, the Prophet Daniel (Chapter 10) had to pray twenty-one days with fasting before the angel of the Lord was able to defeat the 'Prince of Persia', a demonic principality. The angel told Daniel that he was heard by God the very moment he prayed and the angel was sent to him carrying a message. Now God lives in the third heaven (we learn this from Paul who was caught up to the third heaven in 2 Corinthians 12), the demonic principalities, or rulers of the air control the second heaven, and the earth's atmosphere is the first heaven. Therefore the angel had to fight his way past the Prince of Persia and also the Prince of Greece. We can see from this that there are ruling spirits in the demonic realm who have dominion over nations and their leaders, which is why we have to pray.

We know that we are of God, and the whole world lies under the sway of the wicked one. 1 John 5:19

God is not withholding any good thing from us but there are spiritual forces who oppose God and hinder God's answers coming to us.

For we do not wrestle against flesh and blood, but against principalities, against powers, against the rulers of the darkness of this age, against spiritual hosts of wickedness in the heavenly places. Ephesians 6:12

In 1 Thessalonians 2:18, Paul writes that he, Silvanus and Timothy wanted to come to Thessalonica but Satan hindered them from coming, and in chapter 3 verse 10 he declares that they prayed night and day exceedingly so that their way was made clear. Therefore Satan hinders, blocks our way, and blocks God's answers coming to us, and so we have to pray that all hindrances are removed. I am not saying every unanswered prayer is due to demonic forces as many times the problem is due to mind-sets that we have formed. For instance, it is difficult to receive healing from the Lord if you are convinced that He is teaching you something through your suffering. These mind-sets are strongholds that have built up over time, but thank God, praying in the Spirit and meditating on God's Word are both mighty weapons that will demolish them! (2 Corinthians 10:5). Some things take little prayer, whilst other things can take days, months and even years of prayer.

If we are praying for someone's salvation and they are very stubborn, it may take a while to pray through. God never overrides a person's will but he can send someone that will preach the gospel to that person in a way they can receive. The important thing is to pray and leave it to God to work out the details. This is called resting in God after having prayed, committing and trusting all things to Him to obtain the required result.

Jesus was baptized by John the Baptist, and at that moment the Holy Spirit came upon Him. In Matthew 4, the Bible tells us that the Holy Spirit then took Jesus into the wilderness to be tempted by the devil. He fasted and prayed for forty days and nights and broke through the power of Satan and defeated him. It was after these forty days of prayer and fasting that Jesus entered into His ministry. He had broken through in prayer first before He went out to minister to the multitudes.

Now it came to pass in those days that He went out to the mountain to pray, and continued all night in prayer to God. Luke 6:12

Ministry will fail if it's not backed first in prayer. Luke 6:12 describes how Jesus prayed all night, one of the reasons being that he had to choose twelve Apostles and He needed to know the mind of God; immediately following his night of prayer He chose his twelve Apostles, including Judas who would betray Him. Before we have to make major decisions, it is good to take time to pray and seek the mind of God. We may have our own ideas but it's best to get the mind of God who knows the future!

4

Why Tongues?

There are many situations we face in life and we simply do not know how to pray. Some things are way beyond our ability to bring about change and in such cases we pray in unknown tongues (languages). There are known tongues (Acts 2:11) given at times, but usually we pray in unknown tongues, and when we pray in unknown tongues it can sound like mumbo jumbo because our mind does not understand what we are saying, but God does! The scripture says in 1 Corinthians 14:14 that when we pray in an unknown tongue, our spirit prays but our understanding is unfruitful. The Apostle Paul says in verse 18 and 19 of the same chapter,

> I thank God I speak with tongues more than you all; yet in the church I would rather speak five words with my understanding that I may teach others also, than ten thousand words in a tongue. 1 Corinthians 14:18,19

For hundreds of years tongues was assumed to be either a gift that had passed away with the Apostles or a work of the devil, but it is God who gave us tongues in the first place and Jesus said it was a sign that would follow those who believe in His Name (Mark 16:17).

Tongues will only cease when we see Him face to face (1 Corinthians 13:12). In Romans 8:26, we are told that we don't know what to pray for as we ought, but the Holy Spirit helps our weaknesses and intercedes for us with groanings that cannot be uttered, according to the will of God. The word 'helps' here means literally that the Spirit 'takes hold together with us against'. This is something the Holy Spirit does together with us, not apart from us. When we are praying for a very difficult situation our tongues can be almost like deep groanings or we may weep, and as the burden lifts, our prayer language will become easier and start to flow.

This takes practice and experience, but we have noticed that there is always a note of victory when the battle in the spirit is won. The scripture also states that when we speak in an unknown tongue we are speaking mysteries to God in the Spirit (1 Corinthians 14:2). So when we pray in tongues we are engaging the Holy Spirit who then helps us pray and His perfect will comes to pass because the Holy Spirit knows the mind of God (1 Corinthians 2:10,11).

Why Tongues?

But you beloved, building yourselves up on your most holy faith, praying in the Holy Spirit. Jude 20

Praying in the Spirit edifies us so when you feel down, fearful or full of doubt, pray in tongues and soon you will feel better. Tongues can sound like babblings but there are times they can be wonderfully fluent and quite beautiful. Out of our innermost being will flow rivers of living water (John 7:38).

The note of victory

As I have said previously, for some prayer petitions the note of victory can be achieved within a few hours, whilst for other battles, we can be praying in tongues for days, weeks or even months. The key is to reach a point of victory in your spirit. You will sense peace and joy and a certain knowing or confidence that you have obtained the answer.

One of the most important things needed is persistence. I cannot emphasize this enough. The devil does not give ground easily and we need to keep praying in tongues until we reach that note of victory. You can sense, with practice, that 'knowing' that you've broken through. Sometimes you may feel like singing, laughing or clapping. Such is the mystery of praying in tongues that those who do not have this gift will find it quite strange. We are a three part being, i.e. we are a spirit, we have a soul (mind) and we live in a body. We live in a natural world and yet this natural world is often controlled by what is happening in the unseen spiritual realm. There are angels who help God's children and on the other hand there are demonic spirits out to destroy God's people and hinder the work of God.

For though we walk in the flesh, we do not war according to the flesh. For the weapons of our warfare are not carnal but mighty in God for pulling down strongholds. 2 Corinthians 10:3,4

In Ephesians 6:12 we read that we do not wrestle against flesh and blood, but against principalities, powers, rulers of darkness and spiritual wickedness in high places. The same chapter then goes on to talk about putting on the whole armor of God and in verse 18 we are exhorted to always pray in the Spirit, which definitely includes praying in tongues.

We can pray with the Spirit and we can pray with our understanding, and as I said before, praying in our native language is very limited, but praying with and in the Spirit is limitless. One can literally pray for hours in the Spirit and get the victory without seeing anything or understanding what is going on, but the Holy Spirit knows all things and we learn to trust in the Holy Spirit who is praying through us. Like I said, this is something we learn as we pray and put into practice, and it's not learnt overnight. Once you start to pray this way you wonder how you ever managed without tongues.

In my opinion, praying in tongues is one of the most powerful ways to pray, and it's a gift from God many believers do not use. When you first start praying in tongues you may only manage five minutes at a time, but as you persevere your stamina will increase until you can pray an hour or more every day.

Sharon and I have been praying for many years and in recent years we have prayed at least two hours daily, but then we are in full-time ministry. Half an hour to an hour daily is a good target for a lay person. However, in these last days when the world is getting darker and more dangerous we are finding the need to pray even more. When you are in the heat of battle you need to be constantly praying in the Spirit and communicating with the Lord throughout the day.

As the Apostle Paul said, we should pray without ceasing (1 Thessalonians 5:17). We have noticed that a 'break' in the spirit frequently comes around the one hour mark. We start our prayer time with praise and thanksgiving, then we pray in English and as we feel led by the Spirit we intercede in tongues. We pray for ourselves, our nation, our partners, ministry, health, a hedge of protection and our daily needs. We intercede for every meeting we minister at and for special prayer requests which come to us on a continual basis.

Interceding for others

Because we realize that God knows what is coming ahead, we pray in the Spirit trusting God to take care of us. He can see the future and He can see all the traps the enemy may be setting up and so we pray in tongues daily for His protection and guidance. We pray until we have His peace settling in our hearts and then we know all things are covered until the next day. Sometimes at night or during the day if we have a sense of foreboding or unease we start to pray in the Spirit.

The prayer of intercession is prayed on the behalf of others. Sometimes you will actually feel the same emotions those you are interceding for are feeling. You may feel discouraged or depressed and feel like there's something wrong with you personally. As you pray, these negative feelings will subside. When our spirits are open to God's leading, God will put the burden of prayer upon us.

We often don't know exactly what is happening (though the Spirit can tell you — it depends how good you are at listening), but sometimes we see the disasters on the news and putting two and two together we recognize God was leading us to pray. God is always looking for intercessors He can call upon so that the strategies the enemy is planning somewhere in the world are thwarted, and it's a case of being sensitive.

Sometimes as intercessors, God will wake us up to pray in the middle of the night, even though we don't know who or what we are praying for, but we pray until the burden lifts. At times, a person you know will come strongly to your mind — usually this is the Holy Spirit's direction to pray for them. Though God is Sovereign and all powerful, He chooses to work through His body, the Church, and Jesus delegated His authority to us (Matthew 28:18-20).

He cannot do whatever He wants, because first He will never contradict His Word, and secondly, He has given Mankind freewill, so in order to help people He works through His church and people who will pray. If God could do anything He wanted, He would save everybody instantly (because it is His will that all are saved — 1 Timothy 2:4) and we could all live happily ever after, but that's not how it is. God had to become a man to save mankind because it was through a man called Adam that our relationship with God was lost. That's why God became a man, to die for us and redeem us to Himself.

Nothing happens until someone calls upon the Lord and then He moves. Even Jesus, the Son of God had to pray and

He prayed more than anyone, many times interceding all night. He told us that we should always pray and not faint (Luke 18:1) so we should follow His example and become people of prayer.

5

Fasting

The phone rang and it was someone called Rob. I'd met him briefly and prayed for him in a meeting a couple of years prior and now he was on the phone. He told me he was calling from the hospital after being diagnosed with liver cancer and asked if I would pray for him. He informed me that the Lord had told him to call me and I guess it was because the Lord knew that Rob would need intercessory prayer support.

Many people pray a prayer of faith (Mark 11:24) and wait to see God answer, but I knew by the Spirit that Rob would need much more than that. He was facing a very delicate five hour operation to remove sixty percent of his liver and there was a possibility that it had spread elsewhere.

I began to call him daily and pray with him over the phone, and besides that my wife Sharon and I began to pray in tongues for the upcoming operation.

The 'bilirubin' levels in his liver were at 258. A normal reading should be between 1 and 20. So we prayed fervently that the levels would drop dramatically. They fell consistently and when they reached a level of 58 the surgeon was able to operate. Instead of four days in intensive care, Rob was only there for half a day. Prior to the operation I felt led to do some fasting and I fasted the whole day before he went into surgery.

Rob told me afterwards that he felt he was wrapped around in bubblewrap and was at total peace. Even the nurses commented on his composure and thought he was doing yoga or something. I knew it was the Holy Spirit working through our prayer and fasting. To cut a long story short, Rob was cleared of cancer by the cancer specialist but had to undergo some preventative chemotherapy just in case they'd missed something.

The Daniel fast

Jesus and his disciples often fasted and prayed and fasting is part of prayer. It is not easy to fast and of course I must stress that if you are on any kind of medication or under a doctor's care, I do not encourage you to do any fasting without medical approval or permission. Apart from that, you have to be led by the Holy Spirit to enter into fasting and He will give you the grace to do so. The longest fast I completed was a full fast (only water and tea) for nine days when I was facing a big personal challenge, but there are many kinds of fasting.

Please test your servants for ten days, and let them give us vegetables to eat and water to drink. Daniel 1:12

One of the most popular is the 'Daniel' fast where Daniel refrained from any pleasant foods. You can find details of this fast on the internet. Some people will only eat fruit and vegetables during the Daniel fast and it lasts for twenty-one days, but there are no hard and fast rules to this. Fasting is putting your flesh under subjection and it heightens your spiritual awareness and strength. It does not change God or twist His arm, but it changes you.

Spiritual Authority

Fasting simply means abstaining from food for a length of time. You can also do partial fasts where you eat nothing in the day, just one meal in the evening and this is also quite popular. I did this for forty days some years ago and it's one way of fasting for a longer period. There is certainly power in fasting. In the book of Matthew, the disciples tried unsuccessfully to cast out a spirit from a young boy and so they asked Jesus why they had failed (Matthew 17:14-21).

Jesus replied and said, "This type (meaning this type of demon) does not come out except through prayer and fasting." People who are involved in deliverance ministry often spend time fasting, and again I must emphasize that you must be led by the Holy Spirit. If you are a young Christian and are new to the faith, I would encourage you to consult your Pastor or elder first and submit to their counsel.

Is this not the fast that I have chosen: to loose the bonds of wickedness, to undo the heavy burdens, to let the oppressed go free and that you break every yoke? Isaiah 58:6

Jesus himself fasted for forty days and nights before He entered into ministry and often fasted along the way, spending whole nights in prayer. Some situations require a time of fasting to break the power of the enemy and you will see results manifest. Finally, it is necessary to come off the fast slowly as your stomach will have problems if you gallop through a big meal after days of fasting. Perhaps start with a Daniel fast or a partial fast until you are more accustomed to fasting. All prayer and fasting must be done by the leading of the Holy Spirit. Another type of fasting is putting something aside temporarily that holds great value to you. This would include hobbies, TV programmes, sports and similar. We should also fast from anything that gets between us and God. Smith Wigglesworth once said, "If anything in this world fascinates you more than God, then you don't have what God wants you to have." Fasting is practiced in most religions including those who are engaged in occult practices, so it's nothing new.

The church has lost its power because of the lack of prayer and fasting. In these days of easy Christianity the traditional observances of holiness, prayer and fasting are not being sufficiently practiced. We must follow the example of our Lord and His Apostles and observe days of prayer and fasting to regain our spiritual authority.

6

Prayer for Healing

Perhaps one of the most misunderstood issues is the subject of divine healing. Healing was provided for in the atonement and God has already granted all the healing we are going to need on the cross. Jesus not only died for our sins but He also paid for all sickness and all disease. In Isaiah 53:4-5 (KJV) it says,

> Surely He has borne our griefs and carried our sorrows, yet we esteemed Him stricken, smitten of God and afflicted. But he was wounded for our transgressions, He was bruised for our iniquities, the chastisement of our peace was upon Him, and with His stripes we are healed.

Now there are people who have taught that this is speaking about spiritual healing only and not physical healing. So to answer this question we look at Matthew 8:17, where Matthew quotes this verse saying,

That it might be fulfilled which was spoken by Isaiah the prophet saying: "He Himself took our infirmities and bare our sicknesses."

In this chapter of Matthew, Jesus is seen healing the leper, the centurion's servant, and Peter's mother-in-law. Finally in the evening many came to the house and were healed. The context of this chapter is physical healing, so Matthew is indicating that when Isaiah speaks of the suffering servant bearing our sicknesses and pains, he is referring to Jesus taking our physical infirmities upon Himself. Furthermore, the words griefs and sorrows in the original Hebrew literally mean sicknesses and pains respectively. To confirm this the Apostle Peter writes in 1 Peter 2:24,

Who His own self bare our sins in His own body on the tree that we being dead to sin should live unto righteousness, by whose stripes (or wounds) we were healed (past tense).

For example, in Luke 6:19 the word 'healed' here is *iaomai*. Both the Hebrew word for healed *rapha* and the Greek word for healed *iaomai* are used many times for physical healing in the scriptures.

Healing is a gift

'We were healed' means something happened at the cross. Not only did Jesus pay for our sins on the cross but also for our sickness and pain, which is why when we pray for the sick we use the name of Jesus to command sickness and disease to leave people's bodies. Like salvation, healing is a free gift from God. We cannot earn it nor do we need to beg for it, but simply receive it as a free gift. The most amazing thing I have seen in ministry is that since it's a free gift, even unbelievers, whether they are Hindus, Muslims or Atheists, have been healed and I conclude that you don't have to be a Christian for Jesus to heal you.

How much more should a child of God receive healing, for the Bible says healing is the children's bread! Now healing can be received in different ways and I would suggest you get my book on healing called, *An Easy guide to Healing* for further teaching on this subject. If you want to go more in depth, an excellent book is *Christ the Healer* by F.F. Bosworth. Essentially people get healed by the laying on of hands and the prayer of faith, including the anointing of oil (though it's not always necessary); other times people are healed in a service where the gifts of the Spirit are in operation, but there are many who just find it difficult to obtain their healing and this is where we bring in intercessory prayer.

I encourage people to start seeking the Lord, praying in the Spirit and persevering in prayer. The Lord may show them what the blocks are to their healing and one of the major stumbling blocks is unforgiveness which leads to condemnation. This condemnation will block any healing. Sometimes the Lord will reveal an attitude of unworthiness and again this is pretty common. A sense of unworthiness and guilt stops a believer from receiving from God, but as we start praying in the Spirit, God begins to move on their behalf.

Another obstacle to receiving healing is a lack of confidence in God's willingness to heal. The answer here is to read or listen to good teaching on the subject. Another hindrance is fear. When you are fearful concerning your sickness it is impossible to believe. For many people, healing is a gradual process of weeks, months and sometimes years depending on the situation and what we can trust the Lord to do for us.

God has no favourites

Some people get healed more easily than others from what I

have seen over the years. It seems some people are just very open and receptive to God's intervention on their behalf, whilst others do the same things but do not receive and this is a great mystery. God has no favorites and He does not choose who He will heal and who He won't because healing has already been provided in Christ's atonement.

Breaking Satan's Power

Salvation has been made available for every person in this world and yet billions are not saved because they have not received Christ as their Saviour. However, when we intercede, whether for individuals or nations, hearts are softened and people begin to come to salvation. In western countries there is such a lack of prayer and the spiritual atmosphere is so very dry. In 1 Corinthians 4:4 it says,

The 'god of this world' (Satan) has blinded the eyes of them who do not believe.

As we pray, the power of the enemy is broken and people get saved! Similarly as we pray, the power of sickness and disease is broken and healing manifests. I tell folks never to give up and the doctor's report is not the final answer. We can still look to God. As I write this chapter, this morning I rang my pastor friend whose wife was diagnosed with liver cancer. It was too dangerous to operate and it was hopeless. Her weight had dropped to 98 lbs and the doctors said she would never put on weight. They offered her chemotherapy but my pastor friend knew his wife would not survive this treatment. She was bedfast, unable to do anything for herself. My friend took her home and turned his face to God. He started to pray daily in the Spirit, believing for a miracle for there was no other hope.

For several months he has been praying with the help of others. Today he told me his wife has put on nearly a stone in weight and she is up and about, doing normal things around the house like cooking and cleaning. A healing is manifesting through persistent prayer in the Spirit and standing on God's word. Praise the Lord for He is faithful! We are not talking about one five minute prayer here, but continuous prayer daily, looking to the One who hears and answers our fervent prayers (James 5:17,18). Legally the power of the enemy has been broken. He is a defeated foe and Jesus has won the victory but we have to enforce that victory.

The enemy is pretty persistent and does not leave very easily and in these cases we should add fasting to our prayers. Healing was purchased for us and Jesus was wounded for our healing, so healing belongs to us, yet we need to get the enemy out of the way. In John 10:10 it says,

The thief does not come except to steal, and to kill, and to destroy. I have come that they may have life, and that they may have it more abundantly.

We have to fight for our health, but our fight is not physical but spiritual. Prayer is our main weapon together with the Word of God. Jesus fought the enemy in Matthew 4 with prayer, fasting, and the spoken Word of God. Unfortunately, many do not read God's Word for themselves and rely on one sermon on a Sunday, but we must nourish our spirits, souls and bodies with God's Word. We need to pray for the revelation of our authority in Christ and all that God has done for us and in us.

Never give up

Pray without ceasing, Paul tells us in 1 Thessalonians 5:17. Sooner or later, healing will come if we do not faint and give up. Forgive everyone and bless them and get out of sin which opens the door to the enemy (Ephesians 4:27). Take communion often and walk in the love of God. Cast your cares upon the Lord and trust God for your healing. Don't quit! Keep praying and keep believing and healing will manifest. Of course you will experience emotional ups and downs and in the meantime take medication as directed by your doctor and take it in Jesus' name. Seek the Lord if a prescribed treatment is the right thing for you or not, because not all treatments are good for you, but the Lord knows what you need. When my daughter had a very bad skin condition and it had spread all over, we sought the doctor's help who gave her antibiotics. Four times we went to the doctor but there was no lasting cure.

We kept praying in the meantime and God gave us a word of knowledge to use 'wild oregano' which is a herb with anti-bacterial properties. The doctor said he was washing his hands of my daughter's case as we went the herbal route in this case, but we decided to follow the Lord's guidance (be careful when using alternative medicine - go to qualified practioners). We thank God for doctors and nurses; however the medical profession does not have all the answers, but God does! He has the answer - whether we will get healed miraculously, or whether there needs to be medical or natural intervention. Anyway, my daughter was cured using herbs! Praise the Lord! Seek the Lord, pray always and do what God tells you to do and healing will come.

7

The Rhema of God

One of the most useful things in life is to know what God is saying. One word from heaven can sort out so many problems and give us the turnaround we need whatever we are facing. In the Bible, there are two main Greek words for the Word of God. One is Logos and the other is Rhema. Logos is the message whilst Rhema is the communication of the message. To put it another way, if Logos is the Bible, Rhema is a verse from the Bible. Rhema means 'that which is spoken', and it is important that we follow God's spoken Word to us.

Sometimes when we read the Bible, a scripture we have read many times will light up to us, and other times we hear God speaking a word by His Holy Spirit to our hearts. This is God's Rhema Word. We have God's promise which says, 'My sheep hear my voice and they follow'. So God wants us to hear His voice and follow Him. We see examples of how the early Apostles built the church after hearing and obeying the promptings of the Holy Spirit.

In the book of Acts we see some wonderful examples of this. In Acts 8:26, the Holy Spirit led Phillip to go on the road to Gaza where he met a eunuch of great authority under an Ethiopian queen called Candace. Phillip led this man to Christ and baptized him in water, after which Phillip was translated to Azotus (a type of rapture of the church which will happen when we are caught up together to meet the Lord in the air — 1 Thessalonians 4:17). This was probably how the gospel came to Ethiopia.

In Acts 9:11, Ananias was instructed through a vision to go and pray for Saul (later known as the Apostle Paul) and at the same time Paul was also having a vision where he saw Ananias coming to pray for his eyes, since Paul had been blinded by the glory of God on the road to Damascus. This instruction of the Lord was very important in the salvation and subsequent ministry of Paul. In Acts 10:20 the Holy Spirit told the Apostle Peter to go to the house of Cornelius, a Gentile who had received a visit from an angel, and this angel told Cornelius to call for Peter and hear the gospel from him.

What is interesting is that the angel did not preach the gospel to Cornelius, but instructed Peter to do that. Now the Jews did not mix with the Gentiles in those days and so it was quite a step for Peter to go to the house of Cornelius. Peter's obedience was very important, because he realized that the gospel was also for the Gentiles when he saw the Holy Spirit fall on Cornelius and all the people who had gathered to listen to Peter. The Jewish believers didn't realize that the gospel was for everybody and not just for the Jews!

In Acts 16:6-9 the Holy Spirit forbade Paul from going to Asia to preach the gospel, and then Paul tried to go to Bithynia but again the Holy Spirit said no. Finally Paul saw a vision of a man from Macedonia saying "Come and help us." This direction of the Holy Spirit caused the gospel to come to Europe, which was an crucial instruction for Paul. The early disciples frequently received visions and dreams and heard the voice of the Holy Spirit. We too can hear the Holy Spirit's guidance and God can also give us visions and dreams (Acts 2:17).

However, these things can only happen to Christians who are full of the Holy Spirit and are walking with God. Unfortunately there are people who think they are hearing from God and when nothing materializes they wonder what happened. This is especially true in the area of prophecy. We can all prophesy in part according to Paul's writings and you don't have to be a prophet to prophesy. However, if we prophesy from our minds it will not have any power to change things. In the Old Testament, prophecy was taken very seriously and false prophets were stoned!

In 1 Corinthians 12 we are encouraged to let all prophesy so we may all learn. There are churches that do not allow any of the gifts to operate, and so many Christians remain either ignorant or are too afraid to say what God is saying. On the other hand, there are churches who allow too much freedom to prophesy and then there is confusion. There has to be a balance in these things.

Test the Spirits

I can understand church leaders who don't want 'goofy' Christians prophesying and causing problems, and some of these same believers don't like being reproved. The key is to stay humble and be open to the Holy Spirit. Be ready to accept if you are wrong or are corrected. 'Test the Spirits,' the Bible tells us, to see if these things are of God. Above all, the prophetic word of the Lord must line up with His written Word. For instance, the Bible tells us not to be unequally yoked with unbelievers so the Holy Spirit will not tell us to marry a person who is not a Christian.

I did hear of one case where a lady was told to marry an unbeliever because he would get saved shortly. He became a Christian in a supernatural way on their wedding night as she prophesied, but that is the only successful example I've heard of in over thirty years of ministry.

Prophetic words can also come through the gift of tongues and interpretation. With this gift we see people praying aloud in tongues in church and then someone interprets and we ascertain what God is saying. A real word from God is indeed very precious and saves much time, effort and misery, but our spirits must be exercised by praying in tongues to know what the Holy Spirit is saying. Personally, I am very wary of people seeing things in the spirit about me and the way to discern what is from God, is to know God intimately for yourself.

As a young Christian many years ago, I met someone who had been radically saved in prison when the Lord appeared to him in a vision. He told me that God was leading him to go and minister in Holland and furthermore he said that God wanted me to join him. Since I admired him so much, I gave up my job and went to Holland ahead of him to prepare a place for him. After a couple of months he wrote to me and said that the Lord wanted him to stay in England. I was totally devastated and confused. However, because the Lord knew my heart he turned it to my advantage.

I met a real man of God with whom I connected and this was where I first learnt to flow with the Holy Spirit under his guidance. I was very hungry for the gifts of the Holy Spirit and it was in Holland I began to learn about them, so it all worked out well and eventually I returned to England.

The still, small voice

I never contacted the other fellow again who had led me up the garden path and so I learnt the hard way. If God is saying something to you it's good to have others especially in leadership witnessing also in their hearts and thus you can avoid many pitfalls. A still small voice was what the prophet Elijah heard, and so it is that God's voice is revealed when our hearts are quiet and open before Him. It is difficult to hear His voice in the busyness of daily life, and so often we have to wait on the Lord for days, even weeks, to know His direction.

When we pray in tongues we switch into the spirit realm and it is easier to hear His voice in our hearts. God speaks to our hearts through our thoughts to communicate with us, but it starts with our hearts. He is not a God of confusion and His voice brings clarity, so if at any time you are confused, then you have not heard yet from the Lord. When God speaks to you there will be a result, and things will take place that confirm His Word. He speaks in many different ways as long as we are open and willing to be humble and to repent when we get it wrong.

Lives can be saved, however lives can also be shipwrecked, so there is a responsibility when we start giving out prophecies to people especially prophecies that give specific direction. When you pray in tongues, you are switching gears from the natural to the supernatural.

Tongues are a supernatural gift that you cannot learn, but they are given by the Holy Spirit. We still have not fully tapped into the power of speaking in tongues and God would not give us this gift without good reason. So much depends upon our ability to hear God. Life is full of difficult decisions and we need His guidance and direction especially in these troubled times. I remember the story of a Chinese pastor in the underground church who managed to avoid being caught by the authorities time after time, for the Lord would always tell him when the police were coming and he was always one step ahead. The Holy Spirit wants to lead and guide us even in our daily routine if we will look to Him and be constantly prayerful.

8

Different kinds of Prayer

Praying in tongues is just one of several different ways of praying. Over the years men and women of God have received amazing answers to prayer, birthed revivals and changed nations when they didn't even have the revelation of tongues. The Holy Spirit indwells us all at the New Birth experience (the Bible teaches us that we are the temple of the Holy Spirit), but praying in tongues comes only when the Holy Spirit comes to completely fill or immerse a person and He endues them with power (Acts 1:8, Acts 2:4).

This subject has created much controversy and dissension amongst believers, but the thing to remember is that we are all members of the body of Christ whether we are baptized in the Spirit or not. When we see Jesus he will straighten out all our theology! For many years some Christians have denied this 'second' experience with the Holy Spirit, but now Anglicans, Catholics, Baptists and others are joining

Pentecostals in the prayer for the Holy Spirit baptism. "I will pray with the Spirit and I will pray with the understanding" wrote the Apostle Paul in 1 Corinthians 14:15, and so God will move upon prayers in both known and unknown languages.

Most of our prayers are prayers of petition where we are asking God to intervene in some way. This kind of prayer includes long and short prayers for situations and for people. Sometimes when we hear of someone experiencing difficulty or distress we don't have the time or energy to pray a long time for them. We should never underestimate the power of a short, heart-felt prayer especially in emergency situations.

The Power of Praise

The second kind of prayer is the prayer of praise and worship. When they were in prison, the Apostle Paul and Silas prayed and praised the Lord so loudly that the other prisoners heard them (Acts 16:25). I always say when nothing seems to work, try praising God. When we praise and magnify God, it helps us to take our eyes off our troubles and we start looking to God for the answer.

Therfore by Him let us continually offer the sacrifice of praise to God, that is, the fruit of our lips, giving thanks to His name. Hebrews 13:15

Faith will rise in our hearts as we exalt the Lord over our challenges. Someone said you can't worry and be anxious and praise God at the same time. The best antidote for worry and anxiety is praise! In 2 Chronicles 20:22, as the children of Israel praised the Lord, there was confusion in the enemy's camp and they killed each other. The enemy is confused when we praise God in the midst of our problems and praise declares that we are looking to God for the solution.

Praise can be a real sacrifice in the midst of a severe trial and yet there is great power in praise. King David won many battles because he was a great man of praise and you only have to look at the Psalms to see that, for he wrote many of them. We see in the Lord's Prayer (Matthew 6:9) that Jesus starts and ends this prayer with praise and this should be a model for our own prayer life.

The third type of prayer is the prayer of agreement (Matthew 18:19). If two or three shall agree concerning anything they ask, God will move on their behalf. Why this is so I can't tell, but there is power in unity. We are the body of Christ and the hand cannot say to the foot I have no need for you and so when we come together in agreement, God blesses us. However where there is strife and discord, the enemy manifests every evil work. A house divided cannot stand but a threefold cord is not easily broken (Ecclesiastes 4:12), which implies that when we join together in one accord there is more spiritual strength and the enemy can be shifted more easily than praying on our own.

Believing Prayer

The fourth kind of prayer is the prayer of faith.

> *Therefore I say to you, whatever things you ask when you pray, believe that you receive them, and you will have them.* Mark 11:24

It's what I call 'believing prayer'. This is simply expecting and having confidence that the answer will manifest. This type of prayer seems easy to pray but for many people they can pray this prayer and then worry through the whole time of waiting!

When we add worry to our prayer it is not a prayer of faith but it becomes a desperate prayer of hope. When we pray in faith believing, there is rest in our soul and we can patiently wait for the answer to manifest. For me, I prefer to intercede in tongues for a while, and when I sense I have broken through in the Spirit, I pray the prayer of faith and reach out by faith to receive. There is a time to keep praying, but there is also a time to stop and receive by faith and praise God with thanksgiving until the answer manifests.

The prayer of command is also a prayer of faith — this is the prayer that speaks to the mountains (Mark 11:23) in our lives and the lives of others. This is the prayer that the Apostles Peter and John prayed when they commanded the lame man to rise up and walk in Acts 3:6. It is also the prayer we need to use to take authority in the realm of the spirit.

> *And these signs will follow those who believe: In My Name they will cast out demons...* Mark 16:17

Many times after we have interceded in tongues we will take authority over every evil force, binding it up or casting it out so that it ceases from operating (Matthew 16:19, Luke 10:9). As you can see, different forms of prayer can be involved concerning the same situation. We are only separating them for the purpose of teaching and illustration.

'If it be Thy will'

The fifth type of prayer is the prayer of consecration and dedication.

> *For I have come down from heaven, not to do My own will, but the will of Him who sent Me.* John 6:38

Jesus prayed this prayer in the garden of Gethsemane. Jesus did not want to go to the cross and bear the weight of the sin of the world and He prayed to God the Father to let this cup pass from Him, but then Jesus said, "Not my will but Thy will be done," (Luke 22:42). Over the years people have misused this prayer and attributed everything that happens, good or bad, to the will of God. This has been especially so in the area of healing, and people who have not correctly interpreted the Bible have prayed, "Lord if it's your will, heal so and so." And this is contrary to God's Word. Even if it is our time to die and be with Jesus we don't have to die sick and in pain — we can just depart in peace.

Jesus came to give us life and more abundant life. It is always God's will to heal, for He is the great Healer but because we do not see everyone healed we have come up with a neat solution and said, "Perhaps it was not God's will." Jesus revealed the perfect will of the Father in His earthly ministry when He healed all that came to Him and turned no-one away.

So how does the prayer of dedication work? Well suppose you sense to go to a particular country to be a missionary and there is a lot of opposition, you can pray, "Lord if it's Your will, open the door, or provide the finance or visa. If it's not Your will, then close every door," and so to pray this prayer is appropriate.

Different kinds of Prayer

For as many as are led by the Spirit of God, these are the sons of God. Romans 8:14

Beware however of walking through every open door — our greatest guide to following God's will must be the inner witness in our hearts given by the Holy Spirit. Also when it comes to choosing a job, spouse, and any specific area not covered in God's Word. 'If it be Thy will' should not be used when the will of God is known especially regarding salvation, healing or provision. Because God declares Himself to be Jehovah (Yahweh) Jireh (the Lord is my Provider — the will of God is known for He cares for us and wants to take care of us. The exact manner of His provision is not known, but we can expect Him to meet all our needs. This prayer has probably been the most misused prayer I reckon in many denominations.

There are other kinds of prayer of course, such as the prayer of commitment where we cast our cares on the Lord, and the prayer of communion with the Lord - just being quiet and still in His presence and having fellowship with the Holy Spirit. Personally, I usually wait on the Lord quietly for twenty minutes to one hour daily depending on my schedule. As we wait on the Lord we get refreshed, renewed and we are able to hear God's still, small voice. It's difficult to hear His voice when our minds are full of cares and worldly matters.

To conclude, we can see that though there are different kinds of prayer, they do work together at some point and we can combine different ways of praying at the same time.

9

Pray the Answer

Listening to people pray over the years I've noticed how some believers tell God about their problems when they should be reminding God of His promises. We have been given many promises in His Word and these are what we should pray. We say, 'God I am sick,' over and over again, but this is not what is going to bring us the desired result. Instead we ought to pray, 'Thank you Lord, by the stripes of Jesus I am healed!'

God watches over His word to perform it (Jeremiah 1:12) and His Word will not return to Him void (without fruit — Isaiah 55:11). Constantly people complain and moan about their problems and sometimes this is quite understandable as no-one likes going through stuff, but at the end of the day let's pray God's promises and begin to rebuke the enemy and he will flee. Some Christians don't understand that we are in a war and God is not our problem, it's the devil (or our own foolishness) behind every difficulty we face. If we keep on moaning and praying the problem, it only makes it bigger, but if we pray God's promises and magnify God, the mountain is going to shrink in our minds. God knows all about our tests and trials, and yes, we should at first bring things to His attention, but we cannot keep on doing that. God hears us the first time and most definitely the second and third time but at some point we need to find His promise regarding that situation.

If it is sickness we are facing then we find Isaiah 53:4-5 or 1 Peter 2:24, which describes vividly how Jesus paid the price to purchase our healing and we begin to claim our healing and to resist the sickness or the pain. When I say 'claim' our healing, I am not talking about being arrogant, but rather agreeing with God's word on the subject.

For He Himself has said, "I will never leave you nor forsake you." So we may boldy say: "The Lord is my helper; I will not fear. What can man do to me?" Hebrews 13:5-6

If He has said it we can also say it. Just because Jesus paid the price does not mean it will fall on us automatically like ripe cherries, but we have to fight for it and we can only fight for it if we know God's Word. We need to know His Word, believe it and learn to appropriate what Jesus paid for. It's not easy when our pain or sickness is severe but with faith and patience we can win (Hebrews 6:12). Usually the promises of God do not manifest instantly and sometimes we will go through periods of doubt and discouragement before the light dawns.

God's Word cannot fail

We may not win every battle, and some faithful Christian brothers and sisters have died believing God's word, and yet His Word is still the same — "By His stripes we were healed!" Past tense! A done deal! Jesus healed us on the cross and He is not coming down from heaven to do it for us again for it was finished on the cross. Whatever the problem, we need to know what God has to say about it and pray His promises constantly. We may fail, but God's word cannot fail. Of course, if you are not taught this truth in your church then it's going to be much harder.

If the leaders don't know this truth, then the sheep will be at the mercy of the devil and in the end are confused and blame God for the lack of answers! Praying the answer in the midst of our trials and temptations is not effortless and there are no easy answers, but God's word is true and will stand the test of time. We are who God says we are, and not what our in-laws or neighbors say we are, e.g. Romans 8:37 declares that we are more than conquerors in Christ! Now we may not look like 'more than conquerors' but that's what God says about those who are His children. It also says, 'we can do all things through Christ who strengthens us,' and we have what God says we have, e.g. we are blessed with every spiritual blessing and the blessing of Abraham belongs to us. If we simply go by what we feel and see in the natural realm then we are going to lose.

These last days are dangerous times to live. We have the threat of serious disease, terrorism, accidents and all manner of evil. Instead of succumbing to fear and insecurity we can pray Psalm 91 daily, making it personal by putting our names and the names of our loved ones in the prayer — 'Thank you Lord that we dwell in the secret place of the Most High and we abide under the shadow of the Almighty. We will say of You Lord, "You are our refuge and our fortress: our God, in You we will trust." Surely you will deliver us....' And so on.

We must learn to stand on His Word, which means we need to know what the scriptures say, and not listen to teachers who dilute them! As we meditate upon His promises, His Word begins to take root in our hearts and eventually it will produce the desired results, but this takes time. Just as a seed planted in the ground takes time to grow into a plant, so it is with the Word of God in our hearts. Modern life is instant, especially with social media and instant communication, but the things of God take time, like nature. Keep praying

God's word and in due season you will reap. It's easy to talk about your problems and we all need a dose of sympathy at times, yet it's only faith in God's promises that gets the job done.

Of course we need to be sensitive, and not simply quote the bible to hurting people, but be led by the Holy Spirit always! The Spirit of God never condemns but always encourages. God knows about our troubles before we go to Him and He has made provision even before we were born. That is why we can look to His promises and steadfastly pray them, whilst refusing to look at our mountains whatever they might be! Certainly in our journey of faith we will have many highs and lows, but the Lord knows it all. We may lose some battles but the war was won at Calvary. Amen!

10

Let go and let God

One of the best lessons I've learnt in prayer is letting go of my problems to God. I never knew of this, until I heard a message by Dr. Yonggi Cho of Korea, entitled 'Entering His Rest'. God has given us rest in Christ for the Bible says,

> *Come to me, all you who are weak and heavy laden, and I will give you rest.* Matthew 11:28

Jesus is the great burden bearer, and yet we see so many Christians carrying the heavy load of life's problems on their backs, instead of releasing those burdens to God. You see God only really intervenes when we come to the end of ourselves in our natural strength. This is how some of us have come to Christ. We were tired and weary of life and its challenges, and we came to the end of ourselves, then Jesus came into our lives. Suddenly life became happy and beautiful again, but then slowly we started taking back the burdens we gave to Jesus, and started living again in our own strength. Notice how new Christians are happy and carefree but the older Christians look tired and worn out. I was told to wait until the honeymoon period was over and I too would become like them, tired and weary. 1 Peter 5:7 says,

Casting all your care upon Him, for He cares for you.

I believe God wants us to stay happy and carefree for the rest of our days, if we can only keep giving our troubles to Him, and leaving Him to sort them out. It doesn't mean we are to be negligent of our duties and irresponsible, but it's like someone said, you have a 100lb weight on your back and you have a donkey walking by your side. Why not simply transfer the weight upon the donkey that can easily carry the load and just walk alongside the donkey. So we can walk with Jesus but let Him carry the load, as we continue life's journey by His side.

Easier said than done, but that is how God wants us to be, happy and carefree, and full of the joy of the Lord. I know of a mother who prayed for many years for her daughter who was mentally and socially challenged, for she had a condition called Asperger's syndrome, a type of autism. The girl was in institutions, special schools, seeing doctors and psychiatrists and in special accommodation. Medically her situation was impossible, but the mother prayed for years. We too prayed, and all her church friends prayed for years, but there was no change in her daughter's behaviour.

She would be drunk many evenings, go off in the middle of the night, not understanding the dangers of talking to strangers because she was basically a child in her mind, even though she was twenty years old. Her poor mother grew so very tired from worrying, that in the end she told me she was just going to hand her daughter over to God.

God would have to do the worrying now, because she had come to the end of herself; she could do no more. She was prayed out and had no more strength left to worry. The first miracle happened when she surrendered her daughter to God. The first sign of change started when she stopped drinking and said that she wanted to go to college.

She enrolled in college and some wonderful changes began to take place in her behaviour. God was at work as soon as the mother gave her daughter over to Him. You see, as long as we hold onto our burdens, but are still hoping for our prayers to be effective, it does not work. Our prayers will be hindered because we still are keeping control of our cares and concerns, but we must give them to God. He will not share His glory with just anyone, and He works in His own way. To receive help from God in answer to our prayers, we must give our difficulties over to Him. Someone said, God can't fix it if we keep hold of the problem, but if He has it and we stop meddling and getting in His way, then He can fix it.

Trusting God

A funny story to illustrate this point (related by Dr Cho) — an elder of a church decided one Sunday to go to the mountain top to worship God instead of going to church, because he was bored in church. With a picnic basket he spent the whole day on the mountain praising God and   fellowshipping by himself with God. Anyway, he fell asleep, and woke up to find it was pitch dark. There were no lights on the mountain and he had not decided to stay so long, so he had no torch or light of anykind. Gingerly he tried to make his way down in the dark, but he slipped and started to fall down the mountain slope. He managed to grab hold of a branch and clung on for dear life on the side of the mountain. He called out for help but there was no-one up there, so he called out to God for help. Then He heard God's voice saying to him, "Son, I am here, so let go of the branch and you will be okay." The man replied to God saying, "If I let go of this branch, I will crash and die!" And so God said to him, "Son, do you trust me?" to which the man replied, "Of course I trust you God." Then God said, "If you trust me, let go of the branch." But the man couldn't trust God enough to let go of the branch. So he hung on and hung on and eventually with all strength gone, he had to let go. Amazingly he fell to the ground safely, because he was only a few feet above the ground!

If he could have trusted God, he would have saved himself a lot of pain and heartache. And this is how it is with us, if we can't let it go and give it to God. The reason we can't, is if God fails then we shall be in trouble, so we try to help God solve our problems. But instead we should pray and surrender our concerns to God and let Him work them out while we rest in Him. This is one of the reasons prayers are not answered, because even though we have prayed, we still worry and fret. Daily we need to give things over to Him, and yes, He may tell us to do some things which are different from what we expect. Philippians 4:6,7 says,

Be anxious for nothing, but in everything by prayer and supplication with thanksgiving, let your requests be known to God; and the peace of God, which surpasses all understanding, will guard your hearts and minds through Christ Jesus.

We can give our burdens to God through the Holy Spirit who is our Helper and who wants to assist us and engage with us in life's journey. So yes, we must pray and seek the Lord, but in the end we are going to have to give our problems over to God, for He can solve them when He has them wholly in His hands, while we rest and enjoy our life. That's the carefree life Jesus died for!

11

Prayer for the Nations

I hear many Christian folks complaining about the state of our country. We see how the gay lobby has won successive victories over the issue of marriage, and recently in Ireland over sixty percent of the people voted in favour of gay marriage. We see other laws coming into effect which cause problems, e.g. a nurse was fired from her job because she told a Muslim colleague about her faith. Another Christian woman working for British Airways was fired for wearing a cross at work. Now British Airways allow Muslim women to wear a covering over their heads (a hijab) or Sikh men to wear turbans but a Christian woman was fired!

Unfair, absolutely! Doctors and nurses are not allowed to pray for their patients and have to keep their faith under wraps, and yet in the old days many doctors and nurses were practicing Christians and prayer by the bedside was accepted. This is all persecution by the back door.

Thankfully in this country we do not see the level of persecution that believers suffer in other parts of the world, but neither should we take for granted the freedoms that we have at the moment. At present the minority is given preference, and yes, we must protect the rights of the minority, treating them with love and respect, but they should not impose minority values over the majority. The other point we must realize is that our country is Christian in name only, with many moral boundaries being broken all the time, especially on the internet and on television where violent and sexual scenes are portrayed openly and we don't know where this will end up! What is the cure? Prayer is the answer, and God's intervention through prayer.

If my people who are called by My name will humble themselves, and pray and seek My face, and turn from their wicked ways, then I will hear from heaven, and will forgive their sin and heal their land. 2 Chronicles 7:14

Unfortunately many churches do not have prayer meetings, and those that do are usually attended by only a handful of dedicated people. Many church leaders don't pray openly so the congregation does not pray. If only our church leaders would set the example in prayer and see it as a priority, then the people will follow. Dr. Cho, of the world's largest church in South Korea with nearly a million members would be up early at four o'clock in the morning to go to the early morning prayer meeting. South Korea has lived constantly under the shadow of the threat from North Korea and this is one of the main reasons people have prayed, and God has kept this nation safe from the dictators of North Korea.

Leaders set the standard

Everything begins with the leadership, and when the leaders set the standard and preach accordingly, then the people will do the same. God can only intervene when people pray and if we don't pray we restrict God from operating. There are people who believe in God's sovereignty to the extent that everything is up to God, everything that happens is His will, and we don't have a part to play, but this is incorrect. The Lord's Prayer in Matthew 6:10 tells us that we should daily pray that His Kingdom would come and that His will be done on earth as it is in heaven.

Jesus has given us His name and His authority to subdue and dominate evil forces by His power, and if we don't use His delegated authority things will go from bad to worse. We are the salt of the earth and if we lose our saltiness nothing will be preserved. We are also the light of the world and if we hide our light there will be more darkness in our nation.

We are in the last days and time is indeed very short and there is much to be done.

Millions are in the valley of decision. If men of God are only interested in building their empires, compromising the Word of God and being prayerless, we are indeed in trouble. We cannot blame the government or its people, for the blame lies at the feet of the church. We are so divided, and a house divided cannot stand. Perhaps in the midst of persecution the church will finally take its place and win the spiritual battle through prayer and intercession. In the first letter to Timothy 2:1-2, the Apostle Paul writes,

Therefore I exhort first of all that supplications, prayers, intercessions, and giving of thanks be made for all men, for kings and all who are in authority, that we may lead a quiet and peaceable life in all godliness and reverence.

Bad leaders in government will pass bad laws and we will suffer. History shows us the damage evil rulers can do to previously great nations. Proverbs 25:5 says, Take away the wicked from before the king and his throne will be established in righteousness, and when the righteous are in authority, the people rejoice (Proverbs 29:2). Leaders are busy people and they have a lot to deal with and yet the priority must be prayer. A praying church will survive in difficult times, but a church that does not pray will not be around for long, or if it is, it will be a dead, fruitless church. We are in a spiritual war and we must recognize that our battle is with satanic forces in the spiritual realm (Ephesians 6:12), and not only that, but our weapons are also spiritual (2 Corinthians 10:4). So it's no use complaining about the state of our nation, rather it's time to pray for our country and our government. Our church leaders must set the example in the prayer life of the church and not leave it to a few dedicated old ladies to carry the spiritual burden.

Thank God for the praying women of any church, but prayer is not an option but a priority for every Christian. Men like Rees Howells prayed fervently for the nation during the Second World War and we need more men and women of this calibre. Can you imagine if some of the megachurches of thousands prayed together for our nation, or if every church leader would come together to pray, what a difference it could make! Perhaps I am wasting my breath, and things may have to get much worse before we all wake up to the call of prayer!

12

Conclusion

A praying Christian is one who is looking to God for help. I suppose there are times of crisis in all of our lives when we resort to prayer. When the doctor says there is no hope, then we turn to prayer. Prayer reveals our need for God's intervention, and people who have prayed over the years have learnt to prove God in prayer. Our society demands instant access and we can see that in online shopping, where you buy something with one click (Amazon for instance). With instant messaging via email, text and other technology we have become a society not used to waiting - that's why they call them fast food chains, as they have your meal ready in minutes!

Prayer is slow and can be hard, especially when you don't see quick results and discouragement can set in. God is faithful and He does answer heartfelt prayers, however it's true that some of our prayers remain unanswered.

We must of course pray in the will of God, i.e. we can pray for those things which God has already promised, such as protection, provision, health, salvation and so on. Occasionally my wife and I have experienced apparent failures where someone we've expected to be healed has died instead. These moments can bring disappointment and make us feel perplexed. However, we have come to realize that the problem is not with God — some things we will only know the answer to when we see Jesus face to face.

In other areas we need to find out the will of God. The will of God is found in the Word of God, and we must know His Word so we can pray accordingly. Also in prayer and intercession we have to persevere as there are many opposing forces which have to be subdued by God's angels, who war with us towards a good end. Many prayer failures are simply the result of giving up too soon. People who don't pray much, (and that appears to be the majority otherwise our prayer meetings would be full), have not experienced the fruit of their praying.

Secondly, prayer meetings can be quite boring as you listen to some people pour out their woes, rarely praying positively and probably feeling sorry for themselves. We can't simply pray our problems but rather pray with the Holy Spirit, and this is why praying in tongues is so important. We don't know how to pray for our families' salvation, nor do we know how to pray for our neighbours or our church brethren, but God does. He knows how to reach people with the Gospel. He alone knows the deep needs of various individuals. He knows our future and He alone knows the right timing and the direction our lives should take. The Holy Spirit searches out everything, and as we pray in tongues the Holy Spirit goes into action. When we pray in tongues, we speak mysteries to God and we do not know what is being said but God understands all manner of tongue-talking. To the unlearned speaking in tongues sounds like gibberish, but it's powerful.

Passionate praying

For years church leaders have scoffed at the enthusiastic tongue-talker as being over emotional but what's wrong with a little emotion? We have so many dry Christians praying dry, long winded prayers from the mind rather than heartfelt, passionate praying. Don't get me wrong - praying in tongues can be unemotional too, and no less powerful for it. The proof of the pudding is in the eating, and until you are filled with the Holy Spirit and speak in tongues, you will not figure this out with your head. Praying in tongues does not engage the mind for it comes from the heart. There are so many things we cannot communicate to God, but with the gift of tongues we can pray and worship Him excellently. These days we have big bands in our churches leading worship, with lots of lights and other props and they make a great sound, but how many of these dear folks sing in the Spirit? The Apostle Paul said, 'I will sing with the Spirit and I will sing with my understanding (1 Corinthians 14:15).' Singing in tongues causes us to express our love for Jesus far beyond any words we can express!

Next time you go to church, see if there is any singing in the Spirit - it's so spontaneous and so beautiful. You see people dancing in church which is fine, but there is nothing as beautiful as when the Holy Spirit comes upon someone and they dance in the Spirit — this is pretty rare in most churches because it takes time for the Holy Spirit to come! My hope is that this little booklet will get you started praying in tongues more and more, but the real lessons are learnt as you pray.

I have been praying in the spirit for over thirty years now and have seen some amazing answers, and yet I long for more. I want to be more effective in my prayer life and see more results. In some countries where Christians face persecution and fear for their lives, or don't have the medicines they need, they pray and look to God more. Perhaps in the Western church we are too well fed, and because we have easy access to doctors and hospitals and enjoy the freedom to worship that other nations do not have the benefit of, we don't have the same need. However things are changing even in the West and many Christians coming from overseas are showing us the way in prayer. Let's not leave it too late, let's pray, and let's pray in the Spirit that God's will be done in our lives, in our churches and in our nation. Amen.